MORE INTERIOR MONOLOGUES FROM AMERICA'S FAVORITE PRENATAL PIXIE . . .

Yes, Eggbert fans, it's true—after all these years, our hero is *still* waiting in the wings to make his entrance. Fortunately, he hasn't stopped treating us to his delightful insider's view of life, as this all-new collection of rib-tickling cartoons shows. Eggberta, that charming lady-to-be, is along too, to add to the fun.

So even if you're not an expectant mother, you can get your kicks from the antics of the winsome imps in *Strictly Fresh Eggbert*.

D0733530

STRICTLY FRESH EGGBERT
is an original POCKET BOOK edition.

Books by LAF

Eggbert: Funny Side Up
Scrambled Eggbert
Strictly Fresh Eggbert

Published by POCKET BOOKS

 *Are there paperbound books you want
but cannot find in your retail stores?*

You can get any title in print in **POCKET BOOK** editions. Simply send retail price, local sales tax, if any,
plus 25¢ to cover mailing and handling costs to:

MAIL SERVICE DEPARTMENT
POCKET BOOKS ● A Division of Simon & Schuster, Inc.
1 West 39th Street ● New York, New York 10018

Please send check or money order. We cannot be responsible
for cash.   *Catalogue sent free on request.*

Titles in this series are also available at discounts in quantity
lots for industrial or sales-promotional use. For details write our
Special Projects Agency: The Benjamin Company, Inc., 485
Madison Avenue, New York, N.Y. 10022.

STRICTLY
FRESH EGGBERT

Cartoons by LAF

PUBLISHED BY POCKET BOOKS NEW YORK

STRICTLY FRESH EGGBERT

POCKET BOOK edition published May, 1973

 ───────────────────

This original POCKET BOOK edition is printed from
brand-new plates made from newly set, clear, easy-to-read type.
POCKET BOOK editions are published by POCKET BOOKS, a division of
Simon & Schuster, Inc., 630 Fifth Avenue, New York, N.Y. 10020.
Trademarks registered in the United States and other countries.

I.

Standard Book Number: 671-77642-8.
Copyright, ©, 1973, by LAF. All rights reserved.
Published by POCKET BOOKS, New York, and on the same day in
Canada by Simon & Schuster of Canada, Ltd., Richmond Hill,
Ontario.
Printed in the U.S.A.

1243

STRICTLY
FRESH EGGBERT

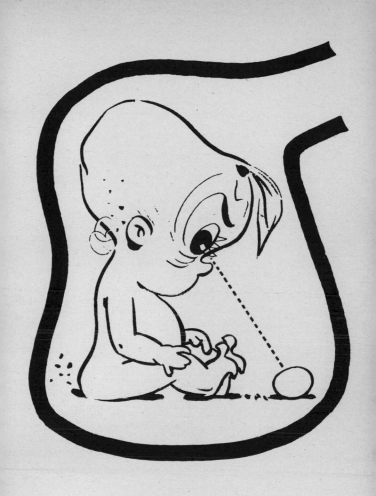

"SHE'S GOTTA BE <u>KIDDING!</u>"

"THE OLD MAN COULD MAKE
A FORTUNE AS A MASSEUR!"

" THERE GOES ANOTHER SMASHED
FENDER ! "

" IF SHE DOESN'T LEARN TO BASTE SIDEWAYS... I'M GONNA END UP A <u>POTROAST</u> ! "

"HOW DID YOU GET HERE? BECAUSE YOUR MOTHER'S DAMN FORGETFUL, THAT'S WHY!"

" THAT'S WHAT SHE GETS
FOR CONSTANTLY MUNCHING
SUNFLOWER SEEDS ! "

"SHE GOT SOAP IN YOUR
EYES AGAIN, HUH?"

" BOY, EVERY DAY IT'S GETTING TOUGHER TO CLIMB THOSE BACK STAIRS ! "

"WHAT THE HELL ARE WE DOING
IN THE VATICAN ?"

" FROM THE DIALOGUE AND HER
SNORTS, WE'RE WATCHING
AN 'X' MOVIE ! "

"SOMETHING TELLS ME SHE AIN'T GONNA HOSTESS THIS FLIGHT MUCH LONGER!"

"STOP JUMPING AROUND! THAT'S
THE THIRD TIME SHE FELL
INTO THE POOL!"

" SO SHE'S GOTTA PLAY THE GUITAR
ON HER LAP, YET ! "

"SHE CAN'T BE LOOKING TOO BAD, YET...
SOMEBODY JUST WHISTLED AT HER!"

"SOUNDS LIKE THE DRIP
IS OVER THIS WAY... "

"LOOK WHO'S SUDDENLY PARADING
FOR WOMEN'S LIB!"

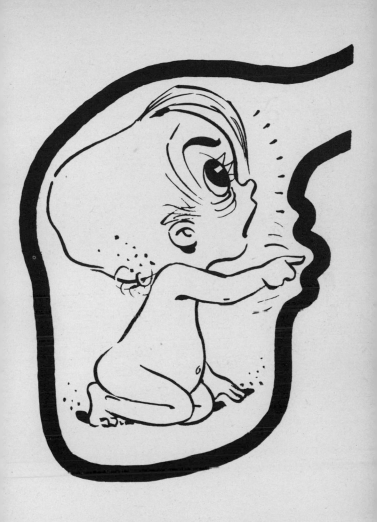

"IT'S YOUR OWN DAMN FAULT...
YOU VOTED FOR HIM!"

"THINK I'D LOOK GOOD
WITH A BEARD?"

WHO CALLED THOSE DAMN THINGS
" HOT PANTS " ?

" WOW! WHERE DID SHE LEARN THOSE WORDS?"

" NO, I DON'T THINK YOU'RE
OLD ENOUGH TO WEAR A BRA! "

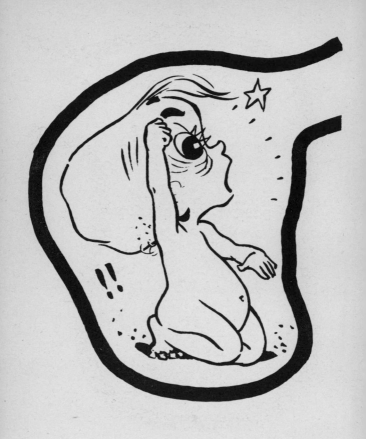

" RIGHT ON, MOM! POWER
TO THE PEOPLE ! "

" I'D SAVE THE OLD MAN A BUNDLE
IF I COULD FIND MY WAY OUT
OF HERE BY MYSELF ! "

"I'D LIKE TA PRA-POZH ... (HIC) A L'IL
OLE TOSHT TA THA GREATES' L'IL MOM
... (HIC) IN THA HOLE UNIVERSH ... "

"IF IT AIN'T MOM...IT'S HER
WATER MATTRESS THAT'S SLOSHING!"

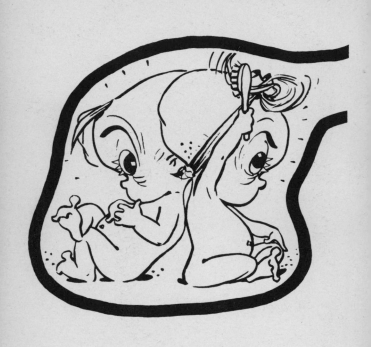

"HOW THE HELL DO I KNOW
IF BLONDES HAVE MORE FUN?"

"FOR THE LIFE OF ME I DON'T SEE
WHAT SHE SEES IN MY OLD MAN!"

" TA HELL WITH THAT 'I'M DUE' ROUTINE!
MY BIRTHDAY AND XMAS AIN'T GONNA
BE ON THE SAME DAY!"

" AW, COME ON, FELLAS...JUST
BECAUSE A NEW STAR'S
IN THE SKY... "

" REMEMBER WHAT I TOLD YA'...
SLUG THAT DOC BEFORE HE SLUGS <u>YOU</u>!"

" THIS IS A HELL OF A TIME TO
DISCUSS WHETHER THEY
CAN AFFORD ME ! "

"THEY SURE GET A GIDEON BIBLE EVERYWHERE!"

" BE HAPPY YOU'RE NOT ENDING UP
SCRAMBLED WITH A STRIP
OF BACON ! "

"NAH! DIDN'T DO A <u>THING</u> FOR ME!"

" CUT OUT THE PANIC! OUR PLANE
ONLY HIT AN AIR POCKET ! "

"THAT'S THE LAST BABY SHOWER SHE GETS _ME_ TO!"

" DAYLIGHT SAVING'S OKAY...BUT I
HATE TO GET UP IN THE DARK ! "

"WATCH WHAT YOU SAY, MOM...
THE FBI MAY HAVE US BUGGED!"

"LOVE THAT BATH POWDER WE USE!"

"SO SHE WANTS TO BE A FOOTBALL PRO...BUT WHY BE THE ONE WHO HOLDS THE BALL FOR THE PLACE-KICKER?"

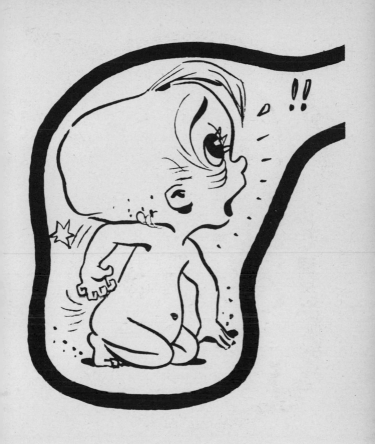

" LAY OFF THE STRAWBERRIES...
I'VE GOT A RASH! "

" YOU'D THINK SHE'D LEAVE THIS
KNIFE-THROWING ACT UNTIL
AFTER I SHOW UP!"

"WE HAVE A SLIGHT INDIGESTION PROBLEM THIS MORNING, I SUSPECT"

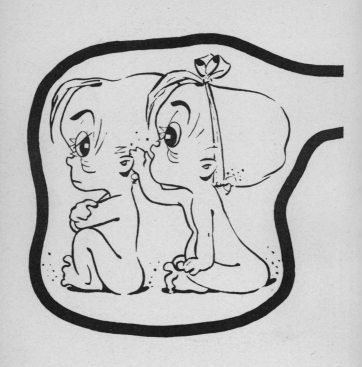

WHATCHA MEAN...
"CAN I KEEP A SECRET?"

"LOSE SOMETHING, DOC?"

"SHE'LL PROBABLY KEEP UP THIS YOGA ROUTINE RIGHT INTO THE DELIVERY ROOM!"

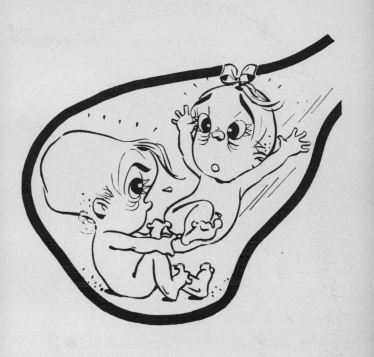

" BECAUSE I SAY YOU CAN'T POKE YOUR
HEAD OUT LIKE A BABY KANGAROO!"

" KINDA BOTHERS ME I NEVER HEAR
A MAN'S VOICE TOPSIDE... "

" COME TO THINK OF IT, SHE HASN'T COME
OUT WITH THAT 'MAKE LOVE-NOT WAR'
GAG FOR QUITE A WHILE ! "

"MUST BE TIME FOR THE OLD BOY
TO GET HOME...WE'RE GETTING OUT
OF OUR BATHROBE!"

" I DUNNO... MAYBE WHEN THEY CAME
TO YOU THEY WERE LOW ON PARTS! "

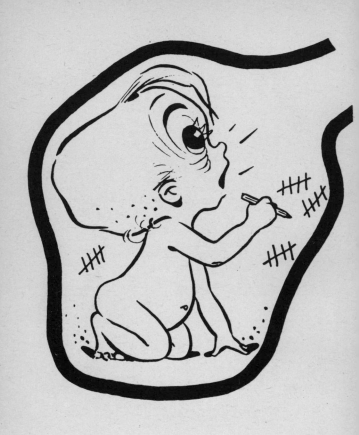

"16 MORE DAYS TO GO, MOM!"

"MAN! JUST CAN'T WAIT TO BITE
INTO MY FIRST HOT DOG!"

"ATTA GAL, MOM! LOCK HIM OUT!
IT'S CROWDED ENOUGH AS IT IS,
DOWN HERE!"

"GET HER! <u>SHE'S</u> TIRED
OF BEING COOPED UP!"

" WOW! SHE'S ON ANOTHER
HOT CHILI KICK AGAIN!"

"ZEESH! IS SHE AWKWARD GETTING
INTO A PANTS SUIT!"

"WHAT A COMPROMISE! YOU THEY
BAPTIZE... I GET BAR MITZVAHED!"

"BET SHE'LL THINK TWICE BEFORE
SHE CALLS HIM TIGER AGAIN!"

" I CAN'T DO MUCH ABOUT <u>THEIR</u>
SNORING...BUT I SURE CAN
SHUT <u>YOU</u> UP!"

" SO, HE HURT HER FEELINGS. WHO
ASKED YOU TO JOIN THE ACT?"

"QUICK, MA...TAKE A COLD SHOWER!
ALL HELL'S BROKEN LOOSE DOWN HERE!"

"IT'S ABOUT TIME SHE ENLARGED
THESE QUARTERS!"

" WHAT A HELL OF A WASTE OF TIME!"

"LAY OFF THAT GAW DAMN PRIMPING!
YOU AIN'T GOIN' ANYWHERE!"

YOU GO "WHIRRR"... I'LL
GO "TICK" AND LET'S SEE
IF DOC PHONES THE FBI!

"THIS AIN'T NO FUN! WISH I WUZ BACK
TO WHEREVER I WUZ!"

" HOPE THERE'S MORE VARIETY TO
THE FOOD OUTSIDE ! "

"SO YOU NEVER WANT TO HAVE
A BABY... I'M CRUSHED!"

" IF SHE CHOOSES BOTTLE FEEDING
WE'RE GONNA MISS OUT
ON A LOTTA FUN!"

"JUST ONCE...JUST <u>ONE</u> TIME I'D
LIKE TO TURN AROUND AND
NOT SEE YOU!"

"GET HER! SHE FEELS NEGLECTED!"

"SHE'S BEEN BITCHY AS HELL ALL WEEK, DOC... THAT'S HOW SHE IS!"

" STICK OUT YOUR HAND AND SEE
IF IT'S RAINING ! "

"WHERE IN HELL
WOULD _I_ GET A BOBBY-PIN?"

"IF I'M <u>THIS</u> SUNBURNED...
WOW! IMAGINE <u>HER</u>!"

" I'LL SURE WELCOME THE DAY
YOU'RE POTTY-TRAINED! "

"FORMULA, HELL! I WANT MINE
RIGHT OUTA THA SPIGGOT!"

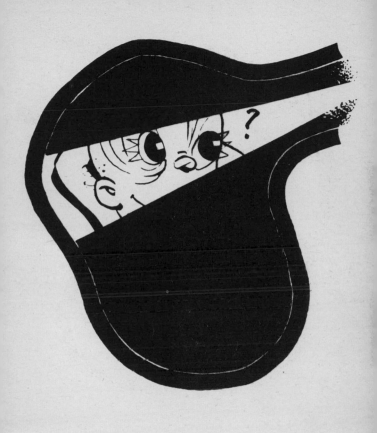

"<u>WHO</u> NEEDS GLASSES, DOC?"

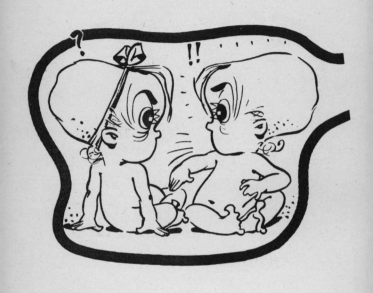

"NO, WE DON'T GO OUT TOGETHER...
AND THAT'S FINAL!"

" I KNEW SHE'D CON HIM INTO
MAKING US LEGAL!"

" I SMELL <u>SMOKE!</u> "

" YEH, YOU STICK OUT YOUR ARM AND
I'LL STICK OUT MY LEG...
AND WE'LL SHAKE HELL OUT OF DOC!"

" LOOKS LIKE ATHLETE'S FOOT TA ME ! "

" STUCK IN ANOTHER REVOLVING DOOR, I BET'CHA!"

"WHAT A PIPSQUEAK! WE'RE CARRYIN' <u>HIM</u> UP THE HOSPITAL STEPS!"

" I KNOW DAMN WELL I MET THAT
BROAD SOMEPLACE BEFORE..."

"FIX YOUR HAIR! WANTA END UP
AN OLD MAID OR SOMETHIN'?"

" SQUEEZE AND GRUNT ALL YOU WANT
I'M COMING OUT WHEN I'M
DAMNED GOOD AND READY ! "

" ALL OF A SUDDEN
I'M GETTIN' HOMESICK!"